# USING THE LAW OF ATTRACTION IN TENNIS

## HOW TO USE THE POWER WITHIN YOU TO TAKE YOUR GAME AND YOUR LIFE TO THE NEXT LEVEL

ALLEN HARTRICH

**author**HOUSE®

*AuthorHouse™*
*1663 Liberty Drive*
*Bloomington, IN 47403*
*www.authorhouse.com*
*Phone: 833-262-8899*

*Published by AuthorHouse 04/16/2021*

*ISBN: 978-1-6655-2218-2 (sc)*
*ISBN: 978-1-6655-2217-5 (e)*

# INTRODUCTION

Before you begin reading this book, I would like to give you some instructions on how to read it. Please start by reading the book all the way through before you try any of the ideas in the book. After reading the book all the way through one time, then and only then should you begin attempting to use the techniques described. By reading the entire book thoroughly one time you will get an idea of all the techniques and hopefully will not let the fact that you have a block with one bother you.

# How did it begin for me?

It all began while I was on vacation with my dog Ella in Tennessee. I had spent the previous six months or so studying the Law of Attraction, Visualization and using your Imagination, reading books like Think and Grow Rich by Napoleon Hill, Ask and It is Given by Esther and Jerry Hicks, The Power of Your Subconscious Mind by Joseph Murphy. I also had started mediating two, sometimes three times a day. I had taken some time off to have some new scenery and think about the next chapter of my life.

We were staying at a small Mountain Lodge resort in Monteagle, TN which is between Nashville and Chattanooga, closer to Chattanooga. It was a nice afternoon in late October and there was a basketball court in back so Ella, and I went out to shoot some hoops and get a little exercise. No one else was on the court so I shut the gates and Ella ran around, often running the ball down and hitting it with one of her front paws or her nose after my many many misses. I remember thinking thank God nobody is watching, I stink! Now I had not actually played basketball for many years, but I literally was missing every jump shot I took, and I was missing them badly. The only shots I could make were basically layups.

So, after missing I do not know how many jump shots, I decided to try something I had been studying and had started working on using visualization and my imagination. So, I dribbled the ball, looked at the basket and then I closed my eyes for about 2 seconds. While my eyes were closed, I imagined myself taking a jump shot with the form of Michael Jordan and my ball going through the hoop nothing but net. So now I opened my eyes and took the shot. It felt great and was nothing but net. I could not believe it! So, I decided I had to try again. So now I dribbled to my left, closed my eyes briefly again, imagined and visualized my jump shot again and exact same result, form felt perfect and shot was nothing but net. At this point I go back to just shooting around and not doing any visualization at all. Only shots I make again are layups.

Before I left, I tried it two more times with the exact same results. By George, this stuff works I thought!

Now I had already begun experimenting with Visualization and Imagination in my tennis game and had been working on it some with my students, but I realized I was not going about it the right way! I would send my students home with instructions to spend time visualizing their strokes but was that enough? It was on this short little get away to Tennessee that I realized how huge using one's Imagination and visualizing could be for their games if truly taken seriously and done correctly. This was going to change the way I teach tennis forever! I will delve a little more into what else I did on the basketball court a little later.

So how does one go about visualization of their tennis game for improvement and to reach their goals or any other sport for that matter? It is primarily the art of using your own wonderful human Imagination. As little children most of us had wonderful imaginations. Most of us were highly creative. Almost every child Imagines what he or she wants to be when they grow up; the President, a Fireman, a police officer, an Astronaut, a professional basketball player, a lawyer, a Supreme Court Justice, or the really special one's (I am a little biased) a professional tennis player. And as kids most of us would tell someone or many people or maybe just our parents our plans. Unfortunately, what usually will eventually happen is one or both of our parents or someone else that we told our dream will tell us to quit being a dreamer; to be "realistic". They make you believe you do not have enough talent, or the family does not have enough money to help support your dream. That you should be "satisfied" to someday have a good paying job, go to high school and make good grades, then hopefully go to college and make good grades and then you will hopefully get a good job that will pay the bills and hopefully you can save a little money and retire someday. They might also tell you that you either must just get lucky or be born with a silver spoon in your mouth if you want to fulfill your dreams! I say that is complete hogwash! If the mind can conceive it, you can achieve it. Your imagination can lead you to greatness if you want it badly enough and allow it to do its job! Remember this, most people are dream crushers! Most people do not really want to see other's being successful due to jealousy and their own fears so you should not let their statements bother you!

Let us talk about the game of tennis for a minute. Mentally speaking, tennis is one of the most difficult and challenging sports to play. It is one of very few sports that is generally one on one, and in order to play at a high level you need to be fit both physically and mentally. Thank about this for a moment, how many sports are there where you can be locked in a dead heat for an hour and suddenly up or down 1-0. This makes the mental aspect of tennis exceedingly difficult but those that learn to handle the pressure well will usually do well in life. You will find that generally good college tennis players generally end up with what most people would say is a successful life in the long run.

The other thing that is very tough for most is the top players train 3-5 hours a day, 6-7 days per week. There's a couple of problems with this: 1. It is a lot of time, 2. depending on who you are training with it can be awfully expensive, 3. That amount of training can be hard on your body over time. Now I am not saying you can be your best without some of that I am just saying there is a better way.

With those issues mentioned above, how can you achieve greatness in tennis if you cannot spend 3-5 hours a day 6-7 days a week training. It does not matter if it is because of time, money or wanting to save the wear and tear on your body, it can be done. One of the most important things that I know is, "You can do it if you believe you can." Now this does not mean you will not have to spend hours on the practice court and working out it just means your practice and workout sessions will be more efficient, therefore they will not take up as much time and won't wear down your body nearly as much. This is where using visualization and your Imagination come into play. Using your Imagination and visualization you can have shorter but better practice sessions, improving your game in shorter amounts of time and learn to overcome mental fear and anxiety on the tennis court and take your game to the next level.

# Chapter 1

## YOUR GOALS AND DESIRES THE STARTING POINT

First things first though. In life, in order to accomplish something what is the first thing you must do? You must have desires and goals......

If you would like to accomplish something you have to determine exactly what it is, you want to accomplish. So, what is your goal? To make varsity on your high school team. Do you want to play for Stanford when you go to college? UCLA? Illinois? Indiana? Do you want to be in the top 100 in the world? Top 20? Top 10? What is your dream? Now you might have to spend some time on this. You probably should spend some time daydreaming about this before you determine your dream. And, you might even have to ask yourself, exactly what do I want to accomplish. What is my primary goal? As mentioned earlier, often we are told by parent's, relatives, friends or even teachers not to dream so much, to be realistic. Do not reach for too much as you will just be disappointed. Most people that do not achieve dreams do not because of one main thing: giving up! Listening to others say, "that's not likely to happen, shoot for something that's more realistic." Be happy if you make the high school team, make good grades, get into college, make good grades, get a degree and a fairly good job. I am not sure about you but that sounds kind of boring to me. And think about this for a minute; if it wan't for people following their dreams and imaginations wouldn't we still be going around in buggies pulled by horses? Would we have computers and the internet? Would we even have electricity in our homes? In the past many if not most inventors or pioneers of new ideas were thought to be crazy! If it is not conventional/rational thinking there must be something wrong with you. You must be "off your rocker".

Every #1 player, every top 10 player, every top 100 players, every Division I College player had a dream first. Without their Imagination giving them the dream would it have happened? I think not! What is the key to your dreams coming true? Harnessing the wonderful power of your Imagination. And you do this through true belief and faith. That is what you are going to learn in this book. How to have enough belief and faith to make your dreams come true.

So, at this point you need to determine what your goal is. Ask yourself, what do I want? Where do I want to go with this? One of the biggest mistakes people make when it comes to their goals: shortchanging their goal because of fear! What if I do not make it? What if I cannot do it? Go into this 'fearless'! What is your dream? If you have a dream that should be your goal. But DO NOT be in a rush! Take your time deciding what your goal is, that is unless you already know. So now decide what your goal is and put it into writing. This is especially important. Spend some time with this. You may want to close your eyes and think about this for a while. Maybe even give it a day or a week to think about this and try to dream about it when you go to bed. But at a minimum close your eyes and daydream about your goal. Before you do this though, ask yourself, what do I want to accomplish? What do I desire to get in life? Now, write it down and give yourself a time frame. When do you want to accomplish your goal by? Also, I suggest you add a shorter-term goal and maybe a medium-term goal if you are younger. If you are going into 8th grade you might have a goal for where you want to be on the high school team as a Freshman. If you are 14 and ranked 50th in your section, you might make a goal to be top 20 in your section in a year and top 100 in the country. Obviously, these are just ideas I am throwing out there. Your goal must be your own goal. Goals are important though. But put your goals and time frames for you goals in writing. And you need to keep them in a place where you will see them regularly. Also, you need to put what you are willing to do to reach your goals. Do you need to work out in the gym regularly to get into better shape? Drill an extra hour a day? Practice with more of a purpose? Play more practice matches? Become mentally stronger. Write this all down and read out load twice a day. Once in the morning after rising and once at night right before going to bed. Hint though, take a little time before you write down what you need to do, and you might add to this over time.

But let us say you long term goal is to be top 20 in the world by the time you turn 22 and let us say that's Oct 2, 2024. So, you will write down the following: By my 22nd birthday on October 2, 2024 I will be ranked in the top 20 in the World in Men's Tennis (or women's). This is my desire, with the help of my subconscious mind, Infinite Intelligence, The Universe, God my Creator my desires will come true. Now the next thing you need to do is read this statement out load twice a day, preferably once in the morning and once in the evening. And when reading these statements, you MUST read them with feeling and emotion. You need to say them with belief! You should close your eyes and imagine yourself with the goal accomplished, the desire or the wish fulfilled. How would that feel. Put yourself in that feeling. This is the Key! Put yourself in the state of mind of the dream being fulfilled. The other key is you want to make it a "burning desire". This is what you WANT! Tell yourself you are willing to do whatever it takes to make it happen. And you HAVE to be consistent. It needs to be twice a day every day. Consistency or a better word to use is "persistency", is the key as well as belief. If you just do it occasionally it will not work. You cannot do it for a day or two then skip a week, come back to it, then skip again and start back up again. It needs to be like eating, you must do it at least a couple of times a day. The more often you say it, and the more feeling you put into it the more you will believe it and the more your subconscious mind will work for you. This will help it to become a burning desire for you.

## Chapter 2

# BEGINNING TO MEDITATE, MEDITATION IS THE NEXT STEP TO TAP INTO YOUR IMAGINATION AND USE YOUR SUBCONSCIOUS MIND.

In order to use your Imagination properly it is important you start meditating on a regular basis. I will get a little more into the why for meditation in another section. But for now, meditation has many, many benefits. We live in an incredibly fast paced and stressful world. There is a 24/7 news cycle which can cause a lot of stress. Personally, I recommend not following the news, but I know for many people that is hard. We also spend an awful lot of time on our phones. Probably way too much for the average person. The average person spends so much time on their electronics that is causes problems for example with how much they sleep. Meditating will help you get that extra relaxing time you need, to turn off your mind and get yourself into the right frame of mind to feed your subconscious mind the information that will help take your game and your life to the next level.

I believe everyone should meditate at least twice a day. There are proven physical and mental health benefits to meditating. People who meditate live longer, are calmer are happier and much less likely to need medication for anxiety or depression or even high blood pressure. There are many ways to go about meditating. A simple way to do so is the following: Get into a relaxed position, either seated with feet on the floor or legs crossed in the Lotus position. Now start taking deep breaths and just focus on your breathing. If you find your mind wondering just go back to focusing on your breathing again. Try to do this for 10 minutes taking very deep slow breaths and exhales. Again, just focus on the breathing. You are trying to completely clear your mind and be thinking about nothing. This is a good start.

Other ways to meditate; You can listen to a guided meditation. There are literally thousands of them on YouTube. Also, there are many good, guided meditations you can buy and download for a small fee. You can also spend 10 minutes slowly repeating a word like "Ohm" continually. Or meta meta (means love) continually. The key is to try it and do it consistently. Do it for 10 minutes twice a day. Once in the morning and once at night before bed. The next best time would be right after eating lunch. If you can 3 times per day is optimal. It is best to meditate when you are a little sleepy. You will find that is when it works the best. Consistently meditate daily for 2 weeks and you will notice a difference in how you feel both mentally and physically. If you currently have anxiety you will notice it going away or bothering, you, much less.

Meditation is the next step in the process of using Imagination and Visualization to drastically improve your game. Be sure your meditation practice becomes a consistent part of your life. Later we will come back to meditating and mix using your Imagination and Visualization with it.

# Chapter 3

## POSITIVE AFFIRMATIONS AKA AUTO-SUGGESTION

Let us digress for a moment. What is the #1 thing stopping anyone from making anything happen? It is Limiting Belief's! Almost everyone has them. "I can't do that." "I just don't think I'll be able to do that." Your limiting beliefs are what you must get rid of. Have you ever heard anyone on the tennis court say "please don't double fault" before hitting their second serve? As a former college and high school coach I can tell you I heard it several times (primarily from high school players). And guess what, often they double faulted. If that is not a limiting belief getting in the way I do not know what is. So, the next step in the process is to use Positive Affirmations otherwise known as Auto Suggestion. You may have heard of this practice or possibly know someone that does this. It is the practice of saying positive statements on a regular basis to make yourself feel better and more positive. It is also a way to get your subconscious mind in the right frame to help you have more faith and belief in yourself. You are trying to tell your subconscious mind something so much that it will come to believe it and therefore take the steps to make it happen. Many people that try this practice get it wrong unfortunately. So why do most people do it incorrectly or get it wrong?

A great positive affirmation you could make daily is: "Every day, in every way I am getting better and better and better." Emile Coue, a French psychologist coined this phrase for his patients in the 1930's. Now most would agree that this is a great statement to make about yourself. Though, most people do not think of themselves getting better and better every day and may have a hard time believing this statement. I know there was a time when I would have had an extremely hard time believing this statement. Now the key to this statement helping you is the following: say it 10-20 times twice a day, morning and night and when you say it you need to say it with feeling and emotion. Get excited about the fact that every day you are getting better in every way. This is how you make yourself believe it and when you make yourself believe it, then it will begin to truly happen. And you must be persistent. It must become part of your daily routine. And honestly, I suggest you look at yourself in the mirror when doing this. Will you see an immediate benefit, no. But if you stick with it you will.

So how will this translate to a better tennis game? You are beginning to train your mind to have more belief in you. Your subconscious mind is immensely powerful and is the key to you becoming a genius at anything: whether it be an inventor, physics, Math or as a great tennis player. Having belief is an exceptionally large part of the battle and it is a must that you get your subconscious mind to believe. So how do you gain that belief? You MUST say the positive affirmation with feeling, emotion and belief. Just like a good actor on TV or in a play or a musical. A good actor or actress often gets so good at their lines and say them with so much emotion and feeling that they get into the role almost like it is real. A good source to check out on this is on YouTube, type in Neville Goddard lectures. My favorite source of these is Brian Scott. He does a really good job on these. Check them out I think you will learn a lot. Listen closely to Neville Goddard's lectures and you will learn a lot about the necessary feeling to get this right.

Next let us take an example of a positive affirmation and put it into terms for tennis use. Let us say you have been making a change in your forehand. You have always hit it too flat and therefore are not consistent enough and make too many errors into the net. So now you have been working on hitting it with more topspin and focusing on hitting specific target areas. Your positive affirmation might be every day I hit my forehand with more and more topspin, it becomes more and more consistent, and I hit my target areas consistently. Now this becomes an affirmation that you say to yourself 10-20 times per day and when you say it I want you to do two other things: 1. say it with feeling and emotion and believe it, because what you believe you will achieve, 2. Close your eyes and Imagine yourself doing just that, hitting topspin forehands that all clear the net by 2-4 feet, have great form and land in your target areas.

This is where we find out how much you really want it. Most people will try this a couple of times, do not immediately notice a difference in their game and give up. This is where persistence comes into play. Persistence is a trait that I believe all winners and over-achievers have in common. The more you do it the more you will believe it is true. The more you will believe that truly is the case with your forehand. The more persistent you are the more it will feel like reality to your subconscious mind and that will make it real. Many people give up because they think what if it does not work. You must just stick with it and keep doing it just like instructed. He or she who is persistent enough will eventually get what they want. So, the question is, how badly do you want it?! Your persistence is the factor that will determine if you succeed or fail. Luke 18:5 "yet because this widow keeps pestering me, I will give her justice. Then she will stop wearing me out with her perpetual requests." So, she is persistent and finally receives justice because of her persistence. How come maybe 2% of the population succeeds and 98% fail? 98% of people give up very easily, only 2 % are truly persistent. Napoleon Hill in "Think and Grow Rick states that "unrelenting persistence" is the key! And, so many people would rather not try because of their fear of failure. The only way to utterly fail is to not give your best effort. But again, the biggest reason for failure is the feel of failure. You have not failed until you quit! But just like the widow in Luke 18 if you are persistent you will eventually get what you want or desire! Think about Michael Jordan; he did not make his high school basketball team as a freshman but instead of giving up like a large percentage of kids in the exact same situation would have, he worked harder, got in as many extra workouts as he could, and the rest is history. He became probably the best basketball player in the history of the game. Have there been maybe better athletes, quite possibly, but I do not think any of them were as persistent. And everyone knows that Michael Jordan had a "burning desire" to be the best. But without his unrelenting persistence it would never have happened. And I bet that he spent a lot of time dreaming about his goals and desires. This is how he realized what he needed to do to obtain them!

Pete Sampras, Roger Federer, Rafael Nadal, Novak Djokovic, the main thing they all have in common: persistence! And I can promise you this, they were also dreamers first. They had to imagine being #1 or one of the top players in the world first.

Thomas Edison failed 1000's of times before he invented the light bulb. So, those were not failures, they were steps on the way to success. I can promise you this, he had a burning desire to get it right. And he had to be persistent! I cannot over emphasize persistence too much. It is one of the main keys to being a winner in life. Please do not give up on affirmations when they do not work immediately. Like anything else they take time and practice. It takes some time for your affirmations to line up with your subconscious mind but with persistence they will. So, do not give up on them. I almost did! I am so glad I did not because had I given up on then I would not be writing this right now. And my life would not be anywhere near as great as it is.

# Chapter 4

## GOING DEEPER INTO THE MEDITATION PROCESS

Now let us talk a little more about your Meditation practice. This is a particularly important part of the process. I suggest you wake up 10-15 minutes early every morning to mediate. This is the best time to mediate because you will still be a little sleepy so your conscious mind will have a hard time getting in the way. Your mind will be in what is called the "Alpha State". So, you wake up 15 minutes early, either sit up with your back against the headboard or wall, sit with your feet on the floor or sit in the Lotus position. Now just take very deep breaths, inhaling and holding it for several seconds then exhaling very slowly. While doing this count backwards form 100-1 slowly and while counting backwards visually see each # like it is on a screen in the room in front of you. You should also have your eyes closed but look upwards into your eyelids at a 20–30-degree angle. Do this for 10 minutes focusing on breathing and counting backwards and then after getting to 1 count 1-5 and do it a little quicker and now you are up and ready to go. Remember, if you catch your mind wondering just gently bring it back. It is okay! You need to make this a habit. Do it every morning. Decide what time you must get up to have time and make sure you are up. This is a must! There is no better way to get your day off on the right foot!

Next let us talk about meditating before bed and using your Imagination! Most people when they think of meditation picture a Buddhist monk with his legs crossed chanting Ohm constantly. I will admit when I was younger that is exactly how I would have pictured it. Now we are going to go into more depth on meditating and how you can use it to improve your game. So right before going to sleep get into a very relaxed position. It could be lying in bed or sitting with feet flat on floor or in the Lotus position. Now take some deep breaths. Really breath in deeply and breathe out slowly. So now as you are doing it try to completely relax your body from the top of your head all the way to your toes and I suggest you think about relaxing every major body part in your mind. Another good technique is to squeeze all your muscles as tight as you can and hold it for 15-20 seconds then just release. That will be total relaxation.

The first week you do this I just want you to work on Imagining and visualization. So slowly count backwards from 50-1 and in your mind picture each # as you say it in your mind. Visualize it as best you can. Next imagine a piece of fruit in front of you, a banana, an apple, an orange, a watermelon, does not matter but try to visualize every bit of the fruit as vividly as possible. Now imagine yourself taking a bite out of it. Try to imagine the taste and what it looks like after you take the bite. Something to realize, for some people this will be easy, for others it will not be so easy. Just try it for a while. Stick with it for a bit. I will give you another method a little later in case you are one of those people that has problems doing this. But in the meantime, continue to picture as vividly as you can. As you are finishing up in your mind repeat the statement: Every day in every way I am getting better and better and better. And as discussed before, when saying this statement say it with emotion and feelings. As much as possible. This is how you believe it, emotion and feelings. Again, this cannot be over emphasized; feel it! Believe it! The more emotion you can say it with the better. We will get back to meditation again a little later. But I suggest you practice this for at least a few days or maybe a week before going to the next step on meditation.

## Chapter 5

# GRATITUDE, THE ART OF BEING
# THANKFUL AND WHY IT IS A MUST!

The next lesson to learn is the lesson of gratitude and being thankful. Having gratitude will help bring you farther then you could ever imagine. First things first. If you can play tennis regularly. If you can have a nice tennis racquet or racquets, you have much to be grateful for. If you can take lessons from a coach that knows what he or she is doing you have even more to be grateful for. If you are part of some free program with a coach that knows what they are doing you have much to be grateful for. Most are not so lucky. Tennis is known as a "Country Club Sport" or a sport for the privileged for a reason, it is not cheap. Unfortunately, very few people spend time focusing on gratitude.

I am here to tell you that focusing on gratitude is one of the most positive things you can do with your life as well as one of the most helpful in the long run. The great thing is it is amazingly simple; take 5 minutes out of your day to focus on what you are grateful for. Here are two ways to do this: 1. spend 5 minutes per day writing down things you are grateful for. Or spend 5 minutes per day looking at yourself in the mirror saying things you are grateful for. The amazing thing is most of us do not even realize how much we must be thankful for. The air we breathe, the beating of our heart, our home, our car, the food we eat, our family, electronics, a pet, your parents, your grandparents, siblings, sunshine, tennis courts, the money you have, vacations you go on, tournaments you can play; there are so many things we must be grateful for. The thing is many if not most people focus on negatives and forget about positives. Focusing on the positive will make your life so much better and easier. It will make you a happier person and being a happier person will have a major effect on your life and where you take your game. You may write or say the following: "I am grateful for: the sunshine, my awesome tennis racquet, my coach that cares about me and my improvement, I am thankful for my loving parents that take care of me, the air I breath, God's (Infinite Intelligence) love for me, my friends, that I am able to play this wonderful sport, that I am able to have healthy food to eat, that I have the energy to play this sport, that I have perfect health! Say these things with passion and conviction! After a few weeks of doing this you will notice a real level of positivity in your life. You will find yourself happier and in a better mood most of the time. It will be hard to bring you down. After you get used to doing this for a few weeks I want you to take it a step farther. You are now going to mix this up a little bit. You will continue to write or say the things that you are grateful that you have but you will now mix in things that you are grateful now even if you do not quite have them yet. Your goal is to play #1 on your high school team? After you write down or say a few things add in I am grateful that I am now the #1 player for my high school team. To be top 20 in your section? I am grateful that I am now ranked in the top 20 of my section. It feels so good to realize my goal. I am so grateful that I am receiving a scholarship to, name whatever school you would like to attend. Mix these things up with all the other things you are grateful for and continue to do this. This will help in your belief and belief is the biggest part of the battle.

## Chapter 6

## ADVANCED MEDITATION; COMBINING MEDITATION WITH YOUR IMAGINATION.

Now on to the next step in using Meditation in this process. We are going to take meditation to the next level. The best time to use your imagination is when you are meditating so let us get into it. Say you have been working on your topspin serve, now it is time to work on that topspin serve off the court as well.

First time you do this I suggest right before sleep at night. Get comfortable, take some deep breaths and in the process relax your scalp, relax your forehead, relax your neck, relax your mouth and tongue, relax your back, relax your chest, relax your abdomen, relax your thighs, relax your calves, relax your feet, relax your toes. One more thing; tighten the muscles in your body as much as you can for about 30 seconds and then relax. You will suddenly feel really relaxed. Now continue to take deep breaths but now I want you to visualize yourself on the tennis court. Try to focus on seeing yourself on the tennis court as best you can. See three orange cones in each service box. Now imagine yourself practicing your topspin serve. As vividly as possible imagine the entire motion, the toss, the contact point, the follow through, picture the ball leaving the racquet landing close to one of the cones and bouncing extremely high like a good topspin serve would. As you are doing this it is important that you have some emotion. You are trying to get in a state like this is really happening. You are excited because you are hitting topspin serves just like you want. Spend about 10 minutes doing this. Again, do it with the feeling like it is really happening. It is the key. Feel it, feel it, feel it. Smile, be happy, feel like it would if you did it on the court. I cannot stress this too much!

Before the first time you do this, you might want to watch a YouTube video or two of someone hitting topspin serves with perfect form. You could also watch your coach if you have one hit some perfect top spin serves and try to save it in your mind. This should help you with the visualization process now you just have to imagine it being you. And I can not overemphasize you are putting yourself into the "State" of this happening right now. You are using your imagination in the most vivid way possible. Your topspin serve really is this good. If you follow these steps and stick with it, you will see improvement in your topspin serve at a much greater rate than without. But again, you cannot do this for 5 minutes, for one night and expect it to work. I mean at some point this may resonate with you so much that a 5-minute session might make a difference, but a certain amount of consistency will be necessary, especially in the beginning. And again, you are trying to be in the state like this is happening, you feel like you are doing it. Eventually your serve will be just like your Imagination. You will be hitting topspin serves that will drive your opponent's crazy! Getting weaker and weaker returns off your serve which will just continue to increase your confidence.

Let us look at another way to use your imagination to help further your game. Example: Ted has a guy named Mark that he just cannot seem to beat. Ted has played Mark 10 times but has lost every single time. The last 6 matches were all awfully close, but Mark pulls it out every single time. By now Ted has a block. He knows that he should be able to beat Mark, but because he has not gotten a win, in his mind, primarily his subconscious mind, he cannot beat Mark. On the other hand, if he beats Mark it is possible, he will never lose to him again. I believe it is time for Ted to use his Imagination as a weapon to finally get that first win against Mark and take his game to the level where he will have the edge in their head-to-head matches. It is now time for Ted to get into his meditative state. I believe it is best as before he does this right before sleep or right as waking up in the morning. Ted will get relaxed focusing on his breaths and relaxing all major parts of his body from the top of his head to his toes. Now in his mind he will vividly imagine himself playing against Mark. In his imagination he will picture himself playing the almost perfect match. Running Mark all over the court, hitting his target's, winning most of the points and see himself winning match point. While doing this the idea again is to have it be so vivid that he feels like he is in the "state" of it happening. He wants to feel emotion while it happens. The feeling is the secret to making this reality. Have emotions, feel it. Feel good about it! Ted has probably been losing to Mark because subconsciously he does not believe he can beat him. The idea is to believe subconsciously that he can beat Mark. When finishing the Imagination, he should state with feeling: "I am so grateful that when playing Mark, I now walk off the court with a victory'. State this a minimum of 10 times. I suggest you do this meditation at least twice, but I also suggest you make the statement at least 10 times twice a day until the next time playing the specific opponent. Again, in his Subconscious mind Ted does not believe he can beat Mark. He must make his subconscious mind believe he can. Once it does, he will.

# Chapter 7

## SETTING INTENTIONS, AN IMPORTANT STEP IN THE PROCESS

How should you prepare for a practice session that you are about to have or a match that is happening in the next hour or so? You need to have the proper Intent for your session or your match. You need to set your Intention out loud. On your way to your practice session or right before your practice session make the following statement out loud 2-3 times: I intend to have a high-quality practice session today where my game improves and I have the best attitude possible, every time I practice my game improves and I get closer to being at the next level. If there is a particular shot, you are going to be working on you might put that in your intention statement. When you say this statement give it a certain level of feeling and emotion. Believe it is true and decide this is what is going to happen. This type of statement is particularly important. It helps to get you in the correct state of mind before your practice session. You will get so much more out of your practice session because of the statement. What if you are about to play a match in an hour? I intend to play the best match possible today, giving my best effort and having the best attitude possible. I see myself enjoying the match and things going my way. Things are always going my way on the tennis court." This will help you go into your match with a good attitude and should help you to maintain a good attitude during the match. Setting intentions are an important part of sports and of life. I used to tell friends of mine they should do this about things in their life and they would tell me I was crazy. Funny thing is these were the people that seemed to always run into the most problems. And they wonder why? Sometimes in life you must be willing to try things outside of your comfort zone. Just because in your objective mind is seems like BS does not mean with some work it won't make a difference in your life.

Make your "intention statements" a habit or ritual and you will see a difference in how fast your game progresses and I genuinely believe it will help you get over anxiety you might normally have in a tennis match.

Let us Summarize what we have learned so far:

1. Have a dream or a goal. Write it down. Make it a "burning desire". This is an especially important step in the process.
2. Begin the process of meditating. Making it twice a day habit. This will have multiple life benefits for you.
3. Positive affirmations. Get your mind in the right place. Remember: Everyday, in every way I am getting better and better.

4. Go deeper into meditation, working on visualization while meditating.
5. Be grateful, show gratitude and see where this takes you.
6. Advanced Meditation tools: Imagining your reality while meditating. Change your reality by using your imagination.
7. Setting intentions is another enormously powerful step that you cannot afford to miss. Be sure to make your Intention statements another habit you stick with.

# CHAPTER 8

## DIGGING DEEPER INTO YOUR GOALS

We are now going to go back and talk about your goal setting again. What was your goal? To play #1 for your high school team. To win a state championship in singles or doubles? To play Division I? To play for a specific Big 10 or Big 12 School? To play for Stanford. Or is it to play on the tour and be top 100? Top 20? Top 10?

Let us talk about other goals. Do you want to have a 4.0 GPA and feel like you are smart enough but for some reason only have a 3.0? You study for your test and feel like you are ready but when it comes time to take the test for some reason you cannot think of answers you know but after the test think of some of the answers you missed? Well, we are going to talk about all these issues.

Let us say you live in Indianapolis, IN and your goal is to play for Indiana University in Bloomington, IN. A Division I school in the Big 10. What are some things you should do besides just work hard to achieve this goal? I would start by going to IU to watch one of their matches, or maybe even a couple of matches. When you are there be observant. Watch the top players play closely but also be observant of the surroundings. Pay attention and take a mental picture of the courts, the environment around the courts, the campus.

Now, when you go home you have some imagining doing. When you go to bed you are going to do your meditation and involve your Imagination but this time you are going to be imagining yourself playing college tennis at IU! So, get yourself in that relaxed meditative state we discussed earlier right before you go to sleep. Focus on your breath and then go through focusing on relaxing the different parts of your body from head to toes. Now you are going to begin to imagine what it would be like to be playing college tennis at IU. See yourself out on the court playing a match and being coached by the coach at IU. Picture yourself having the time of your life as you win your first Division I and Big 10 match at IU. Try to be as vivid as possible. The goal here is to put yourself in the "state" like it really is happening. You want to have some emotion and feeling. Get emotional as you are hitting great forehands and great serves in your first college tennis match. See your teammates and maybe even some other kids from the University cheering you on. How good does it feel? See your parents and how proud of you they are as you win your first match at IU. I cannot stress enough how into this you want to get and how important you do it when you are in a slightly sleepy state. Eventually you will probably dream about this as well. This is your subconscious mind at work I suggest you do this every night for a week. Your subconscious mind will take over and lead you to what you need to do to accomplish your goal. One of the key's though is you will occasionally get feelings on something you are supposed to do. Follow your gut!

This is your Instinct or 6^th sense, and you need to listen to it. It is your subconscious mind doing its thing. I cannot emphasize enough how important it is that you listen and follow through to the best of your ability. If you do not follow through eventually your gut will quit talking to you and you probably will not reach your dream.

Grades? Make affirmations about how well you know the information. Picture yourself getting test's back with A's on them. You might even do a meditation on it. If you studied it, then it is in there somewhere and your subconscious mind can bring it out so now you need to find it and believe me if you make yourself believe it than it will happen. This is the key get the belief! Your subconscious mind will make anything happen that you push on it enough with positive emotions.

Let us digress for a minute. What if you have an amazing forehand? An amazing serve? A great backhand? Wicked volleys and an exceptionally good overhead? But you just cannot seem to win the big points? You lose a lot of close games because when it becomes your advantage you just cannot handle the pressure and lose the point. Or when you get into tie breakers you just cannot pull them out? This is a problem for many tennis players. So, what is the solution is it just play more matches and hope and pray you figure it out? That could work but there is definitely no guarantees, I say you get your imagination involved. Let' your subconscious mind take over and you will see guaranteed results. First thing first on this situation. Let us think of a positive statement to make. "Through divine order and my subconscious mind, I now win the important points of my important matches". Say this statement with conviction, feeling and emotion. The idea is to believe it! You say but how do I feel it and believe it? Have you ever known someone that lies so much that they honestly believe their own lies? I think we all have met at least one person like that in our life. It's unfortunate but they tell them so much that they believe them and the key to believing it is consistency` So now we will use this consistency to help overcome this mental block of winning big points. We are also going to meditate about this. Let us do this again before bed. Get into that semi-sleepy state. Also get into your relaxed position, whether it be sitting in a chair with your feet on the ground, sitting in the Lotus position, sitting with your back against the wall or headboard in bed or lying-in bed. Now start taking very deep breaths, expanding your diaphragm and just focus on your breath for a minute. Now keep taking deep breaths and picture yourself on the tennis court. You are down 5-6 and it is your opponent's advantage. Vividly imagine yourself winning the point and bringing it back to deuce. Now you go on to win the next two points to tie it at 6-6. Feel emotion, get excited, be in the state like it is truly happening. Now you in the tiebreaker down 5-6. Picture yourself playing the perfect point to tie it up at 6-6. Now picture your self winning the next two points to win the tiebreaker. Get excited, be emotional about the fact that you just won this set after being down set point twice Get in that state like it is really happening. Now repeat a similar situation for the end of the second set. And again, make it as vivid as possible. See it, live it! I suggest doing this night and morning for a week then just just assume it is done. You are now the best player at playing the big points. You know this and will affirm it to yourself daily. It is important you use plenty of auto suggestion with this as well. "I play my best tennis on the big points." I see myself coming through with my best shots on the tennis court when it is the most important." Say it till you believe it!

What if your goal is to play on the tour and be in the top 20? How do you train your mind to get ready for that? Let us get into it! First things first and this was mentioned earlier; every player that ever became a top 10 player had a dream about it first. I can guarantee you that no one that made it to the top did not dream about it first. So, do not ever let someone tell you are stupid for having a dream. Dreamers are the people that change the world. Every single inventor was a dreamer. Nikola Tesla was a dreamer. Henry Ford was a dreamer. Thomas Edison was a dreamer. Steve Jobs was a dreamer. Benjamin Franklin was a dreamer. Every single person that signed the Declaration of Independence was a dreamer. Anyone that made the history books was some type of dreamer. Obviously not everyone with a dream goes somewhere with it (nor are all dreamers good, Napoleon was a dreamer and I guess Hitler and Stalin were also dreamers so certain types of dreamers obviously are not good) but dreamers do something with their dreams if they "believe them." That is the key again, belief. Think about a 3- or 4-year-old kid. What do they do a lot? They use their imagination and to them it is a real as the world we live in. This is how you want to be with your dreams. Believe them. A good reference for this you can find on YouTube is Dr. Bruce Lipton. Watch some of his videos, very worthwhile.

So, if you want to be a top player dream about it as much as possible. Picture it every day. See yourself in your mind (use your imagination) playing matches at the professional level and winning them. When doing so get excited, be emotional. Get the feeling of the state of it happening. Talk to yourself about how happy and thankful you are that you are in the process of reaching your goal, whatever it is. Make this a habit, something you do regularly and then "believe it is true". This is the key, 'believe it is true". This is faith. Hebrews 11:1 Now faith is the assurance of things hoped for, the conviction of things not seen, Mark 9:23 "Jesus said unto him, If you can believe, all things are possible for one who believes." Believe that you have received it and you will.' Mark 11:24. After a while, your subconscious mind will help to push you that direction. Now this is especially important. You will receive hunches, gut instincts about things you should do. Maybe enter a certain tournament you were not going to play. An urge to spend 10 minutes on your service toss. An urge to go out for a practice session you were not planning on. You might suddenly think you should add 10 minutes of a specific exercise to your daily routine. Out of no where you may run into a coach that would have never worked with you that fits you in. Take advantage of it. You do not know what all it will be but if you listen your subconscious mind will push you toward the right things to do but you must pay attention. Now you might say, but I do not have the money my family is not very well off so it will never happen. That is the attitude of a naysayer, if you decide you want it badly enough the doors will open for you. You must follow your gut instincts and you cannot let other people's negative self talk get into your way. You stay in positive mode all the time and pay attention for opportunities that will present themselves. And believe me if you do this correctly, they will present themselves, who knows, out of no where you may get an offer for a scholarship to an Academy. This could be completely out of no where. But it's happening because of you and your belief. This is your subconscious mind at work with the Universal consciousness, God! Pay attention and take advantage. These things will happen, and they are happening for a reason. If you want to reach your goal you must keep following your gut. Many people that are successful have these habits and do not even realize it. They just trust their gut and follow it! I cannot emphasize enough how important it is you follow your gut instincts. Here is the thing; most people think I don't get opportunities like that.... If that is your thinking you never will. But if you continually focus on your goal, see yourself in a state of having it in your imagination, breaks will present themselves to you. Have you ever known someone that lied so much that they believed their own lies? I think everyone had known or currently knows at least one person like that. Why do they believe their lies? One word, persistence! They have told them enough that they believe the lie. Here you are just being persistent in believing in your goal. If you continually believe in it, do what your gut tells you to do, work hard and follow your gut your persistence will help make achieving your goal possible and will help those opportunities show up. But you must continue to have faith.

# CHAPTER 9

## STAYING AWAY FROM NAYSAYERS!

Onto the next step in achieving your goals using your imagination and visualization. This is something that can be somewhat hard and something most do not think of. You must stay away from naysayers. (This was briefly mentioned in the preceding section.) We have all met them and most people have them in their life. People that tell you: not possible, your dream is too much, you are shooting too high, aren't you afraid of failing? These are the people you must stay away from! And I cannot emphasize this enough! You need to stay away from these people! At least as much as humanly possible!

Why is is so important to stay away from "naysayers"? Well think about it for a minute. You are trying to live in a "positive state" correct? A state of trust. a state of faith. You want your subconscious mind working for you. What happens to your subconscious when it hears a naysayer regularly making negative comments? Comments of lack. Those comments could very well work against you and make your mind doubt your belief and cause conflict. This is exactly what you do not want. You want your subconscious mind only thinking about the positive thoughts. No conflict. So, it is important you do your best to stay away from naysayers. If nothing else, you keep your goals to yourself as much as possible to avoid the naysayers. If one of your parents is a naysayer, you may have to just keep your goal away from the parent. Things can fall into place without the help of a parent. Your discipline and your belief are much more important than the help of both parents. So, if you must keep most of your goals to yourself there is nothing wrong with that if it is keeping naysayers from effecting your thought. If your mind is hit with conflicting thought patterns, on one side you are trying your hardest to fill it with positive thought's, seeing your dreams fulfilled, your goals accomplished but on the other hand you have someone in your life that is constantly telling you, be realistic, you better have a backup plan, what if you fail? Those conflicting thoughts will make it hard for your subconscious mind to do the best it can for you because it will be in conflict because the mix of negative and positive thoughts. You must do your best to surround yourself with people that are also of what you might call a "higher vibration". People that are more positive and believe in going after your goals and dreams.

When you think about it we all know negative people and we all know positive people but unfortunately most of us know more "Negative Nellies" than we know "Positive Paulies". Why is that? Watch the news! I prefer you not watch the news but if you ever watch the news what do you mostly see? Negative and more negative generally. People dying, people protesting, people getting sick, people claiming to be victims. Is anything about any of that positive? Absolutely not! And most people perpetuate what they see and hear.

Dreamers that realize their dreams do not have the time or energy to waste watching a bunch of garbage on TV that will just bring them down. Unfortunately, negativity sells in this society for some reason. It's honestly very sad. And we wonder why only 1-2% of people realize their goals and dreams. Its not because they cannot or because there is not enough to go around. It is because all of the negative energy. The best thing you can do is surround yourself with positive people. These are people of what I call a higher vibration. They lift you up, they do not bring you down. For some this might mean limiting the time you spend with certain people or even spending no time with certain people. If they are negative, or of a lower vibration they will hurt your chances of reaching your goals. If you learn to stay positive enough you will attract those types of people into your life. These people will find you and you will find them.

Right now, as I have been writing we are struggling with the Covid 19 Virus in this country and in most of the world. Why is it so bad? Belief and fear unfortunately. Those things cause people to become sick. During the Spanish Flu stories about the flu were on the front page of the paper everyday. The Mayor of New York went to the papers and ask them to stop devoting so much space to reports on the Spanish Flu and primarily to take it off the front page. When they did this the rates of infection went down very quickly. Once they took it out of people minds people quit believing so much that they would get sick and fewer got sick. If you want good health, think of yourself only in good health. Say positive affirmations about your wonderful health, this is powerful. But if you think negatively about your health eventually you will be sick or have an injury. Keep your thoughts 100% positive about your health!

What can you do to help yourself stay as positive as possible? There are literally 1000's of positive videos on YouTube you can watch and listen to. Spend 30 minutes to an hour a day listening to some of these positive video's and you will notice that they will affect you in an incredibly positive way. A great one to listen to: Neville Goddard, 'The feeling is the secret". The more positive things you surround yourself with, the better you feel, the more likely you are to reach your goals. This is an especially important part of the process and frankly a big reason why most do not reach their goals and dreams! I mean think about it for a minute. How many negative thoughts are you bombarded with by the world today? The world is filled with negativity. But there are also so many positive things; you just must look for them. And when you spend time in the positive you will find your vibration change to that of a more positive person and with that you will help the good to evolve in your life.

On a personal note, how do I know any of this stuff works. Let us just say I had hit pretty much rock bottom before I found it. Pretty much everything in my life seemed to be going wrong. I had let my business go downhill. I was in some trouble with the law. I lost my fiancé. My body was in pain and my mind was in pain. I honestly was not sure what to do with my life. A friend of mine had talked a lot about these positive and inspirational videos he watched. To me that seemed like a load of crap at the time but one day when I was feeling extra low, I thought to myself, why not, it cannot get any worse. I also thought if nothing else maybe I will get a good laugh out of it. So, I watched some

Tony Robbins videos. Then I started watching videos about "The Law of Attraction". After a while I was hooked so now, I started reading Law of Attraction books, and I read and re-read most of them. Esther and Jerry Hicks "The Law of Attraction the Teachings of Abraham", Ask and It is Given. Napoleon Hill, "Think and Grow Rich" and "How to Own your own Mind". I read some Dr. Joe Dispenza, I read books by Dr. Joseph Murphy. I read the book "The Alchemist". I read several Inspirational and spiritual books like "The Power of Now" by Eckhart Tolle. I was not just reading them multiple times I was also listening to the audio versions. I wanted to learn this stuff; I was suddenly hooked. At the end of this book, I am going to have a complete list of recommended books to read and or listen to but some of these books completely changed my life. Most people do not realize that we really do make our own destinies and that no matter what your current situation is, with the right attitude it can be turned around.

Here now is an example of the power of my subconscious mind at work. At the age of 16 I was in a car accident. Well technically I was driving a pickup truck. It happened early in the morning. After sliding off a curve, hitting gravel and spinning a few times my truck came to a sudden stop and my head slammed backwards into the glass right behind me. I was hurt bad, most likely had whiplash, but like a stupid teenager said I was fine and proceeded to get on a bus 2 hours later and then spend 2 hours on that bus on the way to a high school tennis tournament where I played 3 matches and probably a total 5.5 hours of tennis. Then got back on the bus and went home. My neck was very very sore. My mom who is a nurse and was in bed when I left for the tennis match told me I probably should have gone to the hospital that morning. As the years went my neck got worse and worse. I would see a chiropractor, get a little relief but just that a little relief. Then one day I was in my car and got T-boned by a car that was alluding the police. My neck got worse. I started physical therapy, it helped but I still was in pain daily and tasks like driving (especially longer distances) made it worse. I was probably popping my neck 250+ times a day.

And then right before Christmas of 2020 I made up my mind my neck was going to be healed. I had just finished reading "The Power of Your Subconscious Mind" by Dr. Joseph Murphy. I had already been making the statement "Everyday and in Every way I am getting better and better" quite regularly. So now I had to come up with something new. Here it was: "Everyday and in every way my spine grows stronger and stronger, my health gets better and better, I feel better and better and my neck, back and spine all grow stronger and stronger, thank you God, thank you God, Amen. This was my new positive affirmation. I was also doing this right before bed and in my mind seeing myself with my neck in perfect health and mind you it had been 30 years since my neck was in perfect health. Within 48 hours I noticed a difference in my neck. I used to pop my neck so much I could not even keep track of how many times in each day. Some people would ask me if I had a twitch. It was really kind of embarrassing to me at one point in my life. Now my neck rarely needs popping. It really does not bother me at all. At first, I almost did not know how to feel with a healed neck it had been so long. It felt weird having it back to normal. But it was amazing to be able to drive from my home in Greenwood, IN all the way to Bonita Beach, FL without my neck bothering me. In the past I would be in immense pain by the time I was halfway there. This was amazing. And this was all from me using my subconscious mind. If I can do it, you can as well! All I had to do was say it enough and picture myself and believe myself healed and it happened. But, the two main keys were faith and persistence! The first time you focus on changing something it may take quite a while. In the beginning when you start your belief may be low. You must stick with it until your faith grows. This is the magic key. You must have faith and for most people that level of faith will take time. When I started on this journey, I was a little depressed. I had a lot going on in my life and honestly had decided my life sucked. My business was down, I had been engaged and lost it and was just dealing with a lot of personal problems. I honestly was not incredibly happy at all. Then I started reading and listening to everything positive I could. I read the book "The Alchemist" and learned about "personal legends". I read "The Power of Now" by Eckhart Tolle and learned to focus on my life in the now", I read "Stillness Speaks" by Eckhart Tolle. I read "Think and Grow Rich" by Napoleon Hill, "Success Through a Positive Mental Attitude" and "How to Own your Own Mind' also by Napoleon Hill. "Believe in Yourself" by Dr. Joseph Murphy. What I learned though in a nutshell is we all can be happy and achieve our goals, but you can't look to others to make you happy, you have to "choose to be happy". Which reminds me, I also read the book "How We Choose to be Happy" by Rick Foster and Greg Hicks. Life is all about our attitude and our choices. And you must choose to have a good attitude. You must choose to make good choices. But when you choose to be happy no matter what and you decide what you want and that you are willing to do whatever it takes to get what you want; you will notice a big difference in yourself. More energy, a positive attitude, things that use to get you upset you will hardly notice now. Life will "flow". Will things still go wrong occasionally? Of course, there is no such thing as perfection, but by handling things differently, being positive and not letting things upset you or get you down you will notice more of the good and notice a lot less of the bad.

Example: I use to get upset (borderline road rage) when someone would cut me off or slow me down in traffic. My current attitude when that happens: God and the Universe must want me to be slowed down for a reason right now. I do not know what the reason is, but I accept it. That is so much easier on your mind then getting upset. I have had friends ask me what happen to the Bruce that use to handle these things differently? Or do you not just need to get mad sometimes, so you feel better? My response: can you honestly tell me a time when getting mad made you feel better? Do you really believe anger can make you feel better? Maybe you should think about the last time you got mad; did you really feel better from that? Inevitably the answer is no. Many people have this false sense of what happiness is. But one thing is for sure, getting upset and angry will never make you feel better and it does not make you happy. And being generally happy is one of the main key's to getting what you want out of life. Any you also must realize, things do not make you happy, experiences do not really make you happy; happiness is a state of mind!

If you are in good health, have a nice home, good food to eat daily and can play tennis when you want to you have more to be grateful for then probably 95% of people in the world. So, try thinking about why you should be happy and grateful. That will most likely help you be happier and teach you to look at the bright side which is one of the most important things when it comes to achieving your dreams and desires. People that do not have gratitude rarely achieve their desires and dreams. Also, when you think about it do you want to be happy now or sometime in the future? When you do this or when you have that? Many people think, oh when I have achieved this, I will be happy or when I have this, I will be happy. That is not how being happy works. Choose to be happy now and what you will find is things you want will come to you easier. Choose it with Auto suggestion (positive affirmations), Napoleon Hill has another great book, "Napoleon Hill's Golden Rule's", in this book he devotes an Entire chapter to Auto suggestion. Let us take an example of how auto suggestion might help you in your life in general. Let us assume you have anxiety. Anxiety to the point that you are on medicine. I believe and so did Napoleon Hill, that you can beat Anxiety, and most other illness with the use of Auto Suggestion. So, remember the statement "Everyday in every way I am getting better and better"? Let us add to that. "Everyday in every way I grow happier and happier". "Everyday in every way life gets better and better." "Everyday in every way I grow healthier and healthier." Everyday in every way my mind grows stronger and stronger." Everyday in every way my serve becomes more and more consistent. Everyday in every way my backhand becomes better and better. I think you get the idea here. But again, the key is you must make these statements with feeling and emotion. I genuinely believe that just about anybody with anxiety or depression can beat it without drugs using enough positive auto suggestion. It may take time and effort, but anyone can do it. And would you rather get better from positive self talk or continuing taking drugs that most likely have potentially serious long term side effects? I think I know what I would rather do! And if auto suggestion can help people beat anxiety and depression just think of the potential for positive things in your life from auto suggestion like obtaining a better career, succeeding in sports and or more successful relationships. The confidence you will gain will make a huge difference in your life. I do not think there is a person on this planet that would not benefit from positive auto suggestion in their life. Give it a try and you will see the difference. But again, the key is not trying it for a few days. You must stick with it. Be, what was that word again, persistent! It may take some time. In the beginning you may not believe it. Stick with it! Eventually you will! And do not let yourself fall into the trap of thinking negatively again. I know this has already been discussed but I do not think it can be overemphasized. It would not be good for big pharmaceutical companies if everyone did this, but it surely will be good for you and has the potential to change your life in so many amazing ways.

## Chapter 10

# MIXING YOUR AUTOSUGGESTION (POSITIVE AFFIRMATIONS) WITH YOUR MEDITATION.

I want to discuss auto suggestion, positive affirmations and meditation now in further detail now. I passionately believe that auto suggestion and positive affirmations should be done off and on all day. But I also believe you should mix them with your meditation. You are starting a meditation in the morning? In your head while taking deep breaths say 10 times everyday in every way I am getting better and better. Or say your elbow has been bothering you: everyday in every way my arm grows stronger and stronger. My elbow becomes stronger and stronger. This is another one I have used. I was beginning to have elbow problems from hitting strokes and serves in lessons with my better players. In the beginning I was seeing a physical therapist. I would get temporary relief, but it would pretty much come right back after hitting with pace again. I decided to heal it myself with my subconscious mind. While meditating I would say "everyday in every way my arm grows stronger and stronger, my body becomes healthier and healthier. Arm issue solved. College kid I have worked with came back into town and wanted me to work with him. So now I was hitting even harder than before. No arm issues whatsoever. And have not been to PT for months. What if you are working on your serve; everyday and every way my serve is getting better and better, more and more consistent, I hit my target areas more and more consistently and then picture those perfect consistent serves as you take deep breaths. If there is a particular goal you are trying to meet make an auto suggestion for the goal and then see yourself accomplishing the goal while you have you eyes closed meditating. Picture it perfectly and smile and then talk quietly or out loud or just think about it in your mind if you would like about how good it feels to accomplish the goal. How does it feel to finally have that #1 spot on your high school team that you have always wanted? To win the Qualifier for your Sectional tournament. To win your Sectional tournament. If these are goals of yours, they should at some point become part of your meditation. Get in that feeling of the wish fulfilled and now you are on the path to making it happen. Faith and belief are what will make these things happen for you. By implanting these images in your subconscious mind belief will begin.

I realize these are new concepts for just about everyone in sports, but I can assure you if you are faithful and consistent with them, they will work for you. What I cannot over state is the fact that you must remain consistent. I am sure I will have many many people tell me they tried the concepts in this book, but they did not work for them. I would be willing to bet that 99 out of every 100 people making the statement tried for a week, maybe two, did not get the results they expected and gave up. That is not persistence! It takes time for most people to even get use to meditating. For most the first couple of times will do truly little if anything for you. You must stick with these concepts for an awfully long period of time. The longer you do them the more you believe in them. The more you believe in them the more they will work for you! This is what separates winners from losers, the wheat from the chaff. This is why 2% or less truly fulfill their dreams and why 98% do not. Also, why so many people are poor and so few are wealthy! Most people would rather sit around making excuses and blaming someone else for why they have not succeeded. It is much easier than giving it 100% and following the guidelines in this book. It really comes down to people's fear of failure. Most are afraid to give it their all because they think what if I do that all and I fail. Then I really must be a loser. You must put yourself into a success mindset. There is only one way to know if it works; follow it and follow it completely. And, put the time in. It takes time to change your ways, to change your thoughts, it will not happen overnight. Saying "Everyday in every way I am getting better and better and better isn't going to change your life in a day and it probably won't in a week either. That first week you probably will not believe it and you probably will not say it like you believe it. You have to say it like you believe it for it to work. And for most people that will take time and effort. As I write this now, I have student's that I know are not giving it the full effort this takes. Worthy goals require you to give your best effort all around.

# Chapter 11

## I HAVE A DIFFICULT TIME VISUALIZING AND USING MY IMAGINATION, WHAT DO I DO?

When I originally finished my manuscript, I gave a copy of it to my older brother and one of my older sisters asking them what they thought. My older sister is very analytical and detail oriented so I knew she would give me some insights into how a more analytical person would view all of this. One of the first things she said to me was, "you do realize that a lot of people will have a hard time visualizing and imagining things in their minds and you also realize some will just have a hard time with some of your methods like the counting backwards from 100 or 50 method." I explained to her that I understood that and that some of it was not easy for me in the beginning. But I also understand that especially for the analytic, the imagining and visualizing can be a lot more difficult. Here is one more method for this type of person. Let us take an example here and we should start with a simple goal. You are currently ranked #100 in the Nation. This is just example; your current situation does not really matter. Your goal is to be in the top 20 in the Nation. When you go to bed and are getting sleepy you are going to say: "isn't it wonderful, isn't it wonderful, isn't it wonderful that I am now ranked in the top 20 in the Nation! Repeat this over and over again. Next, I want you to picture your mother or father saying this to you: "isn't it wonderful that you are now in the top 20 in the nation". This is something that everyone can do. My suggestion is to do this before sleep and immediately upon waking and do it regularly. This is not something to do for a bit and quit, this is something to do consistently. Think about this for a minute; you have a goal that could affect your life, completely change it. This is something you want to accomplish badly. I think it is worth taking 10 minutes before sleep and 10 minutes in the early morning to try this. Don't you? If you do not, I am guessing your goal really is not that important to you. If your goal is important to you being persistent in something like this will not be that difficult. How badly do you want it? Give this a try and do it again and again and again. Be PERSISTENT!

There are several guided meditations you can find on "the wish fulfilled". One of these might be worth a try to in addition do your affirmation of it being wonderful. If you are having trouble imagining and or visualizing give this a try. Go to sleep listening to one of these meditations. This is a matter of reprogramming your mind. Different methods work for different people, but I am sure if you are persistent one of these methods will work for you! Piece of advice; you can purchase headphones that come in a headband so you can comfortably wear them while you are sleeping. These are perfect for this. You can play the meditation on a low volume, just loud enough to hear and your subconscious mind will take it in while you are sleeping.

Now I will finish by putting together an action plan for you.

How do you put it all together? Your game plan for taking your game and your life to the next level!

1.  Make your goal(s), set down with paper and pen and write down some notes. Before that though dream a bit. Ask yourself, what do I want to accomplish. Dreaming is important! In todays world most people set their goals way too low. Why is that? Fear of not making their goals happen. The way I see it if you are afraid to dream big you never really hit your real goal(s). So, do not be afraid to dream big and take the time to dream before you make your goals. This is a must. This is the only way you will have a definiteness of purpose and really have a chance to go extremely far in tennis and in life.

2.  Begin Meditating! This is especially important! Even if you do not have big goals meditating will make your life better! I believe meditating can change anyone's life. Whether you are a 15-year-old tennis player, an 80-year-old retiree, a 40-year-old executive, a 35-year-old school teacher, 30 year old mom, or a 45 year old working in a factory. Meditation is something I believe everyone should do. But for sports I believe it is an absolute must. So, find a way to meditate that works for you. Just relaxing and focusing on your breathing, saying

Ohm slowly for 15 minutes, or listening to a guided meditation. But find a way that works for you. This is an absolute must.

3.  Start using positive affirmations or auto suggestion. "Everyday in every way I am getting better and better. Auto suggestion is immensely powerful. This is not spoken about much but almost all great leaders of Industry use it. Your mind is enormously powerful! Most people have used auto suggestion but without realizing it in a negative way. Most people have negative thoughts in their subconscious mind and do not even realize it. Using positive affirmations is a way to erase the negative and change to positive. Your mind cannot have both positive and negative emotions at the same time so if you use auto suggestion in the way of positive affirmations on a regular basis you can remove the negative thoughts in your subconscious mind and replace them with positive. This can help all aspects of your game and your life. And be persistent with your affirmations. In the beginning you might have to put reminders on your phone or post it note reminders for you to see but eventually this will come naturally.

4.  Combining Meditation and Visualization, an especially important combination for taking your game to the next level. Spend some time working on visualization while meditating. Next use your meditation time to work on a stroke you have been working on. Then visualize yourself hitting that stroke perfectly while meditating. Try to do this as

vividly as possible and put yourself in the feeling of this is really happening. Follow through on other sessions by imagining yourself beating that opponent you just have not quite been able to beat and then next imagine yourself while meditating reaching that goal of yours. See yourself playing at the college of your dreams or playing on the tour. Do this regularly. When doing this you need to be emotional. Try and put yourself in the state of your goal being fulfilled. It has happened! Imagine yourself winning those big points in the big matches. The 5-6 tiebreaker points, the 9-9 tiebreaker points. See it vividly, in your mind get excited about winning those big points. This will help you so much with anxiety on the court. In your mind you will believe it which is over half the battle.

5. Be grateful and thankful for all the wonderful things you have in your life. Most of us have many things to be grateful for and do not even realize how much we must be grateful for.

6. Advance Meditation: combining your Imagination to work on your game while meditating.

7. Setting Intentions; what is important today? This week? What are you working on in your practice session? Are you traveling to a tournament an hour away? You should set an intention for safe travel. This is also enormously powerful. What intention might you set before starting a tournament? "I intend to play to the best of my ability, to enjoy my time on court and to have the best positive attitude possible." That is a good example, but you should

obviously try to use your own words. But you must have intentions and you should daily say them out loud to yourself.

8. Dig Deeper into your goals! Do some research, check out the environment that might have something to do with your goal(s) this should help with your imagination and visualization process.

9. Stay away from naysayers! This is one of the most important steps but also one of the toughest ones to follow! Test people. Only be 100% positive around everyone you are close to. Anyone that cannot handle that (that is a lot of people) spend as little time with them as possible or if you can, eliminate them from your life. That may sound extreme but too much time with Naysayers will prevent you from reaching your goals because their negative talk will sneak into your subconscious. And what you must remember is most people really do not care about helping you reach your goals.

10. Mix your positive affirmation (auto suggestion) into your meditation. Positive affirmations should be done as much as possible but adding to meditation time can make them even more powerful!

11. Isn't Wonderful, Congratulations and having your wish fulfilled. If you are having a tough time with the basic steps in the Imagination and Visualization process go to sleep thinking about your wish being fulfilled. Imagine someone close to you congratulating you on realizing your goal. Be persistent and you will see things fall into place for you!

How do you really put this all into action? Because the most important thing with all of this if it is going to work for you is that you are consistent! So how do you do that? Make a schedule and stick to it! What is the biggest reason this will not work for you if it does not work? Lack of consistency is why it will not work if it does not work! Which is also a lack of persistence or discipline! Do you want to reach your goals? To be successful? Or do you want to be like most people and eventually just give up? Most people give up because of a lack of persistence and honestly because it just feels easier to them. But if you genuinely want to reach your goals you will now put this all into a schedule and stick to it. And the easiest way to put this into your schedule is to get out the calendar on your phone and now put this all on a daily schedule. If you are going to meditate twice a day you are going to want to get up 10-15 minutes earlier so put this on your calendar for 10-15 minutes earlier than you would normally get up. Same for scheduling meditation for 10-15 minutes earlier than you normally go to bed. In the beginning you will need reminders to tell you for your self affirmations (auto suggestion) as well. Eventually that should become a habit, but you should put it on your calendar as well. Set aside 10 minutes a day for it. Set aside 10 minutes a day to think about what you are grateful for. Put it on your calendar! In "Think and Grow Rich" Napoleon Hill has an entire chapter dedicated to persistence! Think about that for a moment. He has an entire chapter dedicated to persistence! I highly, highly recommend you read "Think and Grow Rich" because I believe it is a book that can help with pretty much all aspects of your life.

Do you really want to reach your goals and make your

dreams come true? Most people want them to come true but generally do not follow through. Believe in them and follow what your gut tells you to do, then watch how far you go!

Do you want help. If you are just starting this journey this can be especially important so join the Tennis and Law of Attraction Facebook group. Be in a group with other's that can hold each other accountable.

# BOOKS TO READ, YOUTUBE PEOPLE TO FOLLOW.

"Think and Grow Rich" By Napoleon Hill
"How to Own Your Own Mind" by Napoleon Hill
"Success Through a Positive Mental Attitude" by Napoleon Hill
"Napoleon Hill's Golden Rules" by Napoleon Hill
"Believe in Yourself" by Dr. Joseph Murphy
"The Power of Your Subconscious Mind" by Dr. Joseph Murphy
"The Alchemist" by Paulo Coehlo?
"The Power of Now" by Eckhartt Tolle
"How We Choose to be Happy" by Rick Foster and Greg Hicks
"The Power of Awareness" Neville Goddard

You can read these books or listen to them on Audio or both but I highly recommend them all. If you want to start with something that is fun and a quick read start with the Alchemist. I think it's a must!

**YouTube**

**Brian Scott (The Reality Revolution) Neville Goddard Videos, Napoleon Hill Videos, Robert B Stone and Jose Silva Videos**

**Josh Togle Neville Goddard Videos** and Napoleon Hill Videos

**Dr. Joe Dispenza**

**Unseen Sereph Neville Goddard Videos**

Many of the books above can be found on YouTube so listened to for free!

# About the Author

Allen Hartrich has been teaching tennis most of the last 27 years ever since playing College Tennis at Division I Monmouth University. He worked for the prestigious Van der Meer Tennis School at the young age of 21 where he worked many classes with the Legend Dennis Van der Meer himself side by side and use to have after work hitting sessions with the master where he would pick his brain. Besides a brief stint in the financial services industry, Allen has been teaching tennis full time ever since. He has been running his own program on the Southside of Indianapolis since 2009.

Printed in the United States
by Baker & Taylor Publisher Services